SHELF

The Meadow

The Grouper's Reef

THE DEEP

The Moray Eel

Poison

The Poison

The Grouper's Hide-out

The Soldiercrabs' Camp

Poison

THE WITHERED PLAIN

LEGEND

Pearl & Seasnails

Finneus . . . . . .

Bert & Soldiercrabs

Bert, Soldiercrabs & Finneus

N

NW   NE

W   E

SW   SE

S

Beyond the ken of mortal men, beneath the wind and waves,
There lies a land of shells and sand, of chasms, crags and caves,
Where coral castles climb and soar, where swaying seaweeds grow,
And all around without a sound the ocean currents flow…

THE SIGN OF · THE SEAHORSE

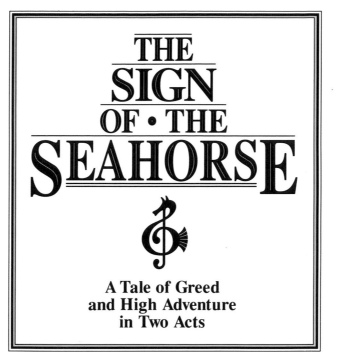

A Tale of Greed
and High Adventure
in Two Acts

Graeme Base

For James

Harry N. Abrams, Inc., Publishers, New York

CAST

PEARL TROUT, a waitress at the Seahorse Café

FINNEUS TROUT, Pearl's brother and a member of the Catfish Gang

MR. TROUT, Pearl's father and proprietor of the Seahorse Café

BERT, a corporal in the Soldiercrab Army

GROPMUND G. GROUPER, a thief, con artist and all-round baddie

A SWORDFISH, the Grouper's lieutenant

TED and STAN, the Grouper's Sharks

The CATFISH GANG, a motley mixture of rough diamonds

A SEASNAIL and his family

A MORAY EEL

The SOLDIERCRAB COMMANDER

Other SOLDIERCRABS

COMBAT LOBSTER 46903

An old and toothless TIGER SHARK

Three ANGELFISH

KEVIN AND THE KIPPERS, a popular Reeftown dance band

Various FINE YOUNG FISH and other REEF-FOLK

STRANGE, CREEPY CREATURES of the Deep

SEAHORSES

And two largely unnoticed SHRIMPS

PRELUDE
The Disappearance of the Seahorses

*In which a spreading poison comes to the Old Reef and all the
Seahorses mysteriously vanish*

Above the ragged reefs they soared, exquisite and serene,
Through slanting shafts of sunlight, tiny jewels of blue and green,
Performing little pirouettes, then sailing side by side:
An everchanging ballet danced upon the turning tide.

Beneath a sweeping canopy of undulating hue,
From wells of limpid turquoise to the deepest midnight blue,
The Seahorse ballet rose and fell – a silent symphony,
Played out against the backdrop of a vast and fragile sea.

Then came a day the sea went dark, the reef began to change,
The coral gardens lost their glow, the seaweed tasted strange.
The shifting ocean currents brought a slowly spreading blight,
And every single Seahorse simply vanished overnight.

ACT I

Scene I
The Seahorse Café

*In which our heroine, Pearl, falls in love with Corporal Bert, and
the evil Grouper pays an unwelcome visit to the Seahorse Café*

The Seahorse Café was the place where fine young fish would meet,
To spend the evening dancing to the latest Reeftown beat.
The rock was hard, the drinks were soft, the chairs were in between;
In short, the Seahorse was the place in which one should be seen.

The café sat upon a knoll, above the ebb and flow,
Unblemished by the poison that was taking hold below.
The band was hot, the place was cool, the atmosphere just right,
And all the fish would bop 'n' hop and boogie through the night.

The owner of the café was a fine, upstanding Trout,
Who had a lovely daughter and a son who seemed a lout.
She waitressed at the café and was cheerful, quick and bright;
But he had joined a Catfish Gang and stayed out late at night.

Despite the shock of spiky hair and earrings in his snout,
Young Finneus was really just your normal teenage Trout.
The Catfish Gang looked tough and mean – no manners, no respect.
But deep inside they meant no harm and dressed up for effect.

The daughter (we shall call her Pearl) would often stop and flirt,
With all the local Soldiercrabs, until she noticed Bert.
He looked the part: a clipped moustache, two eyes, eight boots, one glove.
And Pearl, who couldn't help herself, fell hopelessly in love.

That fateful night when Pearl and Bert first fell for one another,
And she gazed deep into his eyes, first one stalk then the other,
There came a crash, somebody screamed, and in the doorway stood,
The Grouper and his henchfish – it was clear they meant no good.

The Grouper was an ugly fish, with wicked, piggy eyes,
Possessed of bloated appetites, as witnessed by his size.
His pin-stripe suit was tailor-made, complete with matching tie:
Exactly what the well-dressed crook was wearing that July.

A savage-looking Swordfish stood a little to his right,
The kind of thug you wouldn't want to come across at night.
His sidekicks were a pair of Sharks, with dubious IQs,
Who dressed in stovepipe trousers and wore pointy, two-tone shoes.

The Grouper owned the place next door, a sleazy, run-down bar,
Where low-life Slugs and Wentletraps made bootleg caviar.
He'd bought a lot of property in last October's crash,
And ran the sort of businesses where clients paid in cash.

The Grouper said, 'You punks take heed! This warning is for you.
Stay outa this here café or your swimmin' days are through.
I own the only bar in town that's gonna jump and jive.
You come back here again and you ain't gonna stay alive!'

His bodyguards slicked back their hair and circled round the crowd,
As if to dare the customers to voice their thoughts aloud.
Then, roughing up a Seasnail who was less than half their height,
The Sharks rejoined their master and stepped out into the night.

Scene II
Down at the Wreck

In which the Catfish Gang come face to face with the Grouper's Sharks, the Soldiercrabs arrive in the nick of time, and Corporal Bert pens a note to his truelove, Pearl

The Catfish Gang were hanging out down by the local wreck,
Demolishing the rigging on the starboard upper deck,
When Stan and Ted, the Grouper's Sharks, perchanced to happen by.
The Catfish leapt down from the ship and faced them, eye to eye.

Young Finneus was furious. He swam right up to Ted.
'You Sharks are nothing more than stupid villains,' Finny said.
'You think that you're big heroes, roughing up defenseless snails.
Well, let's see how you look with Catfish claw-marks down your tails!'

The Sharks revealed their wicked teeth and grinned a wicked grin.
It looked as though a fearsome fight was shortly to begin,
But suddenly there came the sound of fast-approaching feet:
A company of Soldiercrabs came marching down the street.

They rounded up the Catfish and informed them of their rights,
While Stan and Ted moved quietly away from all the lights.
The area was cordoned off, all trouble spots were manned.
(The Soldiercrab Commander had the crisis well in hand.)

'You Catfish are a rotten lot,' the Crab Commander said,
His buggy eyes surveying them from well above his head.
'I ought to have your whiskers – we can do without your kind.
Now clear off, every one of you, before I change my mind!'

With calculated slowness and impertinent remarks,
The Catfish Gang retreated, looking round them for the Sharks,
But Stan and Ted had disappeared the moment things got hot,
For villains they most surely were, but stupid they were not!

When all the members of the gang had disappeared from view,
The Colonel said, 'Attention men! A message has come through.
A creeping plague is killing off the coral, grey and dead;
Our orders are to find the source from whence this poison spread.'

The Army was to leave at once, all Crabs were on alert,
And at this news a little gasp escaped from Corporal Bert;
For in his heart a crack appeared, a soulful, lovesick pain,
To think that he might never see his truelove, Pearl, again!

The Colonel gave an order and the soldiers wheeled about,
But as they left Bert lagged behind, his mind a sea of doubt.
He longed to see his darling Pearl before he went away,
And tell her all those tender things that parting lovers say.

Just then he heard a rustle in some bushes up ahead,
And from a clump of seaweed poked a spiky mane that said,
'Hey Bert! It's Finny! Over here! I'm hiding in the weed.'
'Dear Finneus!' cried Corporal Bert. 'You're just the fish I need.

'The Soldiercrabs are leaving – in an hour we must depart –
But will you take a note for me to ease my aching heart?
Tell Pearl that I shall miss her every hour of every day.'
So Finny promised Bert he'd take the note without delay.

The other Catfish reappeared as Bert marched out of view,
And held a general meeting as to what the gang should do.
'Those Sharks are getting way too big; let's cut them down to size!'
And so they formed a plan to catch their rivals by surprise.

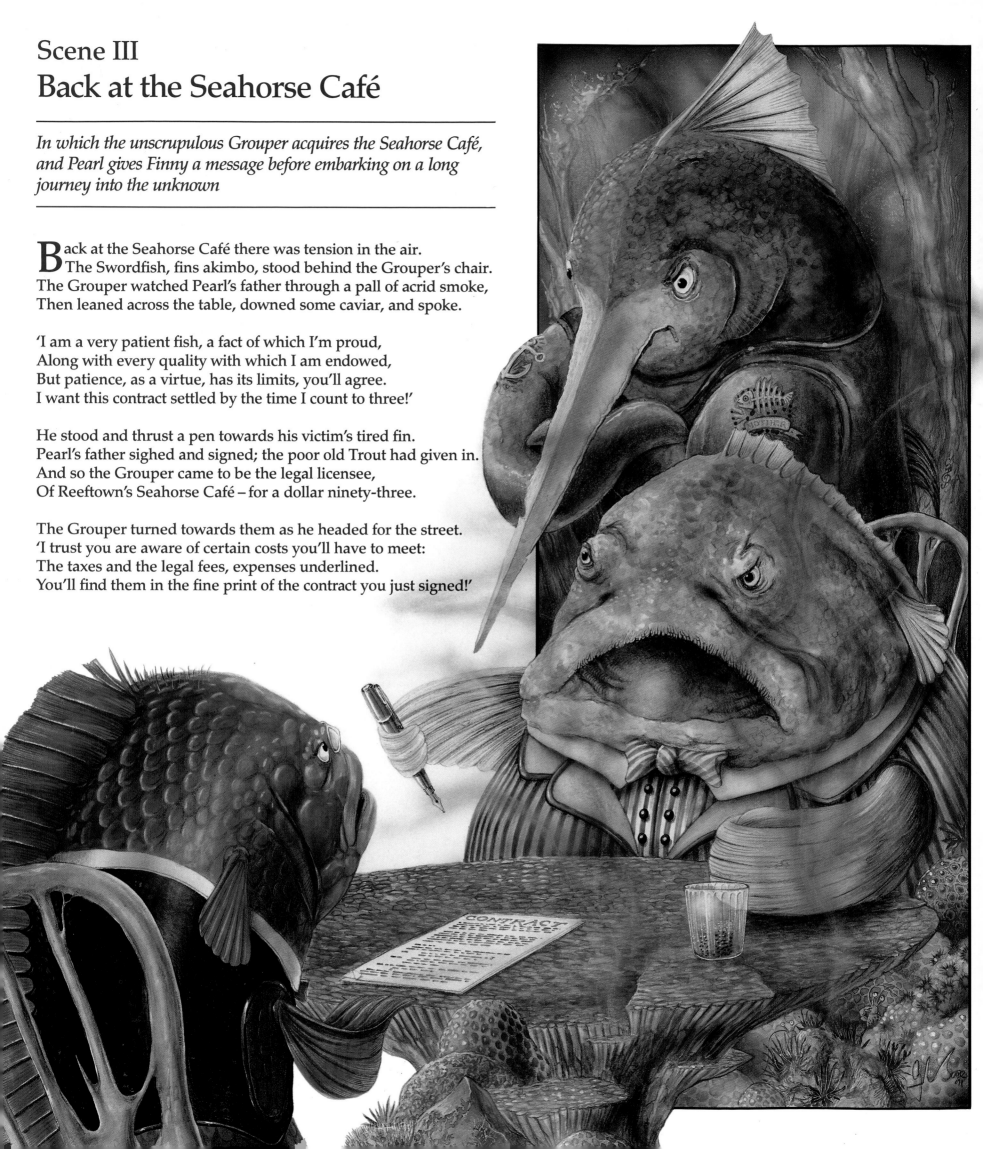

Scene III
Back at the Seahorse Café

*In which the unscrupulous Grouper acquires the Seahorse Café,
and Pearl gives Finny a message before embarking on a long
journey into the unknown*

Back at the Seahorse Café there was tension in the air.
The Swordfish, fins akimbo, stood behind the Grouper's chair.
The Grouper watched Pearl's father through a pall of acrid smoke,
Then leaned across the table, downed some caviar, and spoke.

'I am a very patient fish, a fact of which I'm proud,
Along with every quality with which I am endowed,
But patience, as a virtue, has its limits, you'll agree.
I want this contract settled by the time I count to three!'

He stood and thrust a pen towards his victim's tired fin.
Pearl's father sighed and signed; the poor old Trout had given in.
And so the Grouper came to be the legal licensee,
Of Reeftown's Seahorse Café – for a dollar ninety-three.

The Grouper turned towards them as he headed for the street.
'I trust you are aware of certain costs you'll have to meet:
The taxes and the legal fees, expenses underlined.
You'll find them in the fine print of the contract you just signed!'

The sound of wicked laughter was still hanging in the room,
An eerie echo adding to the general air of gloom,
When through the door burst Finneus, who handed Pearl the note.
She paid no heed to grammar and disclosed what Bert had wrote.

'My Darling Pearl, I must away, for Duty doth require,
I sally forth to unknown parts and dangers dark and dire.
But, through all kinds of Peril, naught shall cause me harm or hurt,
As long as you still love me. Signed: Your Ever-loving Bert.'

'Oh Finneus, what shall I do?' Poor Pearl began to weep.
'For we must also leave tonight and face the oceans deep.'
Then Pearl told brother Finny of the café's awful fate:
Another Grouper's Diner full of Sea-slugs, Eels and Bait.

The dreadful news hit Finny like an anchor from above;
To think that villain owned the place he'd come to know and love!
'I'll not be going with you, Pearl; I have a job to do.
That thieving thug has bitten off far more than he can chew!'

With that he turned and made to go, but Pearl called out his name.
'Dear Finny, what you did for Bert, please do for me the same.
Take Bert this note so he may find the trail that I shall make:
A secret path of seahorse signs to mark the road we take.'

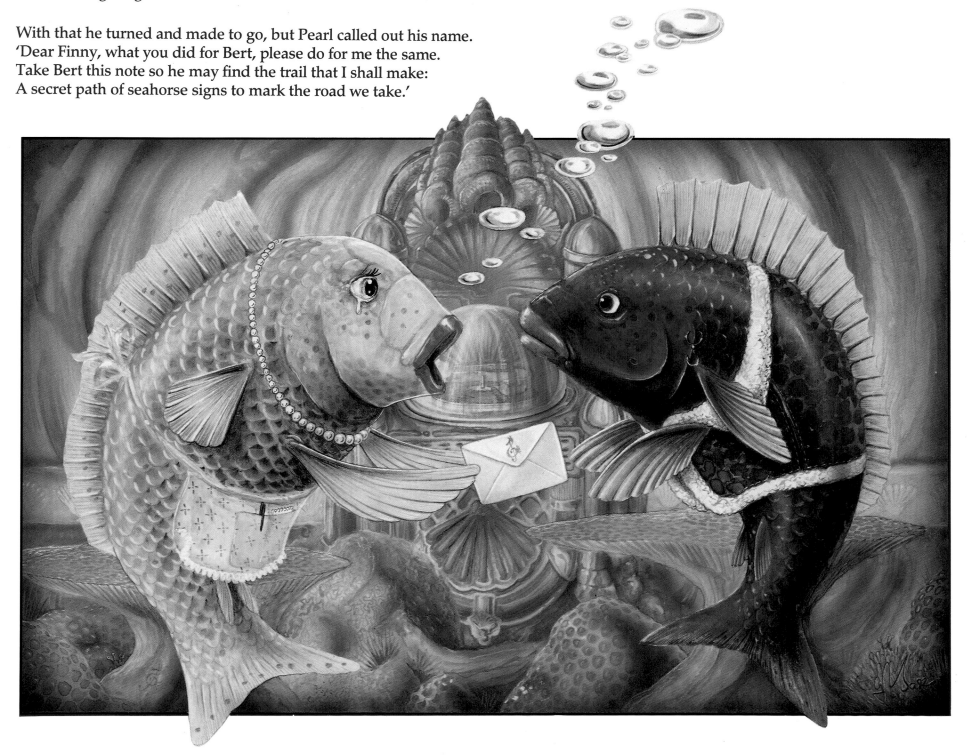

As Finny left to join his gang, and Pearl began to pack,
A Seasnail trundled past, with his belongings on his back.
Behind him came his wife and kids, who numbered twenty-four,
And, as they passed, the Seasnail's voice came wafting through the door.

'This place we used to call our home has really gone to pot.
And now, on top of all the rest, the reef's begun to rot.
When Sharks are free to terrorize a poor, defenseless Snail,
I'd say the situation has gone well beyond the pale!'

Pearl watched the Seasnail catch his breath beneath the café lights,
And grumble to himself about the lack of Shellfish Rights,
Then called to him, 'We too must travel roads we do not know.
Pray tell where you are headed, for we know not where to go.'

He told her of an ad he'd seen in last week's *Seaweed Mail*,
About a distant coral reef with building lots for sale.
'Outstanding Value! Close to Shops! All Coral Fresh and Clean!'
It sounded like a bargain so he'd bought one sight unseen.

The thought of healthy coral, flanked by seaweed lush and long,
Convinced Pearl and her father they should join the Seasnail throng.
So, turning off the flashing lights and slamming shut the door,
They boldly went where no salt-water Trout had gone before.

Scene IV
The Grouper's Hide-out

*In which the Catfish Gang learn of the Grouper's evil scheme to
destroy the Old Reef, but their visit does not go according to plan*

The Grouper's secret hide-out lay a little out of town,
Where stunted weeds grew, sparse and drab, and all the rocks were brown.
From deep within a tangled pile of cars and rusty beams,
The Grouper ran his businesses and planned his fishy schemes.

An old and toothless Tiger Shark was posted by the door,
But from his creaking chair there came a steady, wheezing snore.
The lookout dreamed uneasy dreams, completely unawares,
As seven stealthy Catfish crept across the wooden stairs.

They peered in through the windows, keeping safely out of sight,
And watched the scene within, lit by a grimy, yellow light.
The room was lined with works of art and crates of stolen goods,
That left no doubt the Grouper's gang were rotten robbing hoods.

The Swordfish sat inscribing his initials on a chair,
While Stan and Ted, the Grouper's Sharks, combed sump oil through their hair.
Three Angelfish sang a cappella jazz beside the bar,
As Gropmund Grouper sat and gulped his bootleg caviar.

Then rapping on the table with his jewel-encrusted cane,
The Grouper stood and made a speech, both arrogant and vain:
'This evening's celebration marks a most auspicious day;
A victory for Grouperdom in every wicked way.

'That beastly Seahorse Café will no longer jump and jive.
I'm gonna turn the place into a seedy, run-down dive.
No lights, no stage, no music, no more funky three-piece band –
The fish will stay away in droves, exactly as I planned!

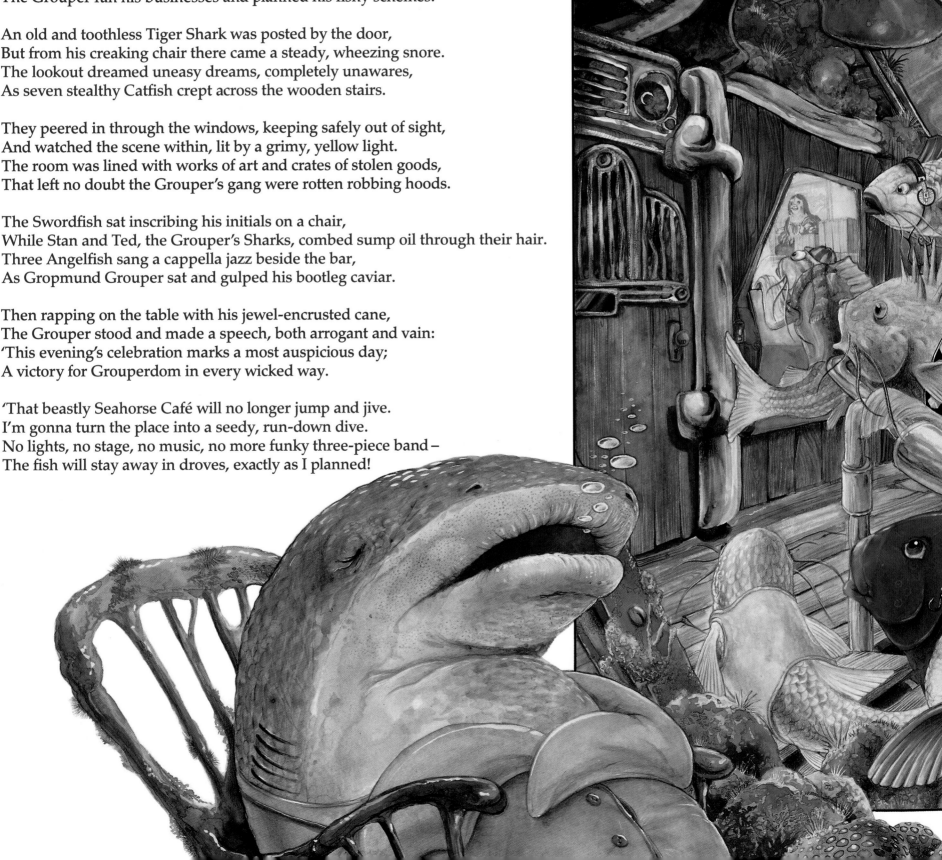

'I bought the Seahorse Café just to watch the business fold.
I plan to see an empty stage, the dance floor bare and cold.
It's part of an ingenious plan, my shrewdest scheme to date,
To make a massive fortune in the field of Real Estate.

'Some time ago I bought a reef and advertised it well,
But what I really needed was some trick to help it sell.
Then from above the poison came, a strange and wondrous sight:
Twelve giant barrels tumbling through a dark and stormy night.

'They came to rest beside my reef, which soon began to die –
It seemed to me a bitter blow dealt cruelly from on high.
But then I put my mind to work and came up with a scam,
To turn my loss to profit. (That's the kinda guy I am.)

'I sent my boys to do a job, a very secret task.
To share the burden round a bit: is that too much to ask?
And so it was the poison spread, as if a tap had turned.
(Which as you know is how poor Teddy's dorsal fin got burned.)

'So now this reef is dying, too; it's looking far from fit.
The citizens of Reeftown know the time has come to split.
They're looking round for somewhere new before it gets too late,
And I've begun to sell *my* reef – at twice the going rate!

'Of course, when selling property, one uses certain jargon,
To raise a bit of interest; make it sound like there's a bargain.
"Outstanding Value! Close to Shops!": these phrases grab attention.
(While minor things like poison somehow fail to get a mention.)

'Some parts of it remain unsold, a coral bed or two.
It's cut my profit down a bit and that will never do.
But all those fish who used to hang around that Seahorse dive,
Will soon be looking elsewhere for a brand-new place to jive!

'And as for all the poison, it is sure to stop one day.
(As soon as Ted goes back and turns the valve the other way.)
I'll wait until the coral beds regenerate, and then,
I'll sell the Old Reef back to them for twice as much again!'

The Catfish, hearing every word, were filled with disbelief:
This Grouper was a good deal more than just a petty thief!
His crime was more than wicked; it was barbarous and mean,
The most outrageous rip-off that the reef had ever seen.

They leapt through open windows and they crashed through ones that weren't,
To teach the Sharks a lesson that would never be unlearnt.
The Angelfish were terrified and darted here and there,
While gutless Gropmund Grouper cowered underneath his chair.

The Catfish gained the upper hand, but victory was brief,
For though the Sharks were beaten, there was still the Swordfish chief.
He made a lunge at Finneus and caught him by the nose,
And wouldn't let him go until the other Catfish froze.

The game was up, the battle lost, the raiders overthrown,
Then Finny saw his chance and made a break-out on his own.
He bit the Swordfish on the fin, dropped smartly to the floor,
Dodged quickly past the startled Sharks and vanished through the door.

END OF ACT I

ACT II

Scene I
The Deep

In which Pearl and her companions journey through the ocean depths and outsmart a hungry Moray Eel

The Seasnails, Pearl and Mr. Trout were far away from home,
In strange, uncharted waters where no Reef-folk ever roam.
Around them towered murky shapes of rocks and cliffs unseen:
The grim, forbidding shadows of a deep and dark ravine.

The little band of travelers pressed onward through the Deep,
Past fearsome, black anemones and fish that never sleep.
And as they journeyed bravely through this bleak and dismal vale,
Pearl carved her little seahorse signs to mark the party's trail.

They came across a fallen rock that blocked the path ahead,
And forced the group to take a less inviting route instead.
Pearl stopped to leave a seahorse sign, but as she drew her knife,
The rock that Pearl was resting on came suddenly to life!

It reared up high above her head, a writhing, snake-like figure,
That looked like some enormous slug, except with teeth and bigger.
Pearl dropped the knife and, leaping back, she gave a little squeal,
For rearing high above her was a great, big Moray Eel.

'My dear,' he said in dulcet tones, 'I really must protest.
You very nearly ruined my expensive satin vest!
And this one is my favorite, so elegant yet plain –
I think I'll have to eat you so it won't occur again.'

He smiled at Pearl, a hungry gleam reflecting in his eye,
But Pearl had kept her senses and she told a desperate lie.
'How lovely!' she exclaimed aloud. 'An Eel has come to dine.
My friend the Killer Whale will be along to chill the wine!'

'A Killer Whale?' the Eel inquired. 'My dear, I think you jest,
And little fish who tell white lies are something I detest.'
But suddenly a roar rang out, from somewhere up on high,
That sounded very much as though a Killer Whale was nigh.

The Moray Eel was most impressed and quickly changed his style,
From 'Ruthless Deep-sea Predator' to 'Service with a Smile'.
'Perhaps I can assist you, Ma'am? It seems you need a hand.
I know these parts extremely well – your wish is my command.'

(That mighty roar was not, in fact, a bonafide Whale,
But just a quick impression by our friend the little Snail.
He'd grabbed a giant trumpet shell and given all he'd got;
A trick that every Seasnail knew but Eels, it seems, did not.)

The Moray Eel was anxious now to make the Whale his friend,
For fear his life might soon come to a most unpleasant end.
And so he told Pearl all about the valley and its traps,
And how to find the secret ways through fissures, cracks and gaps.

He told her how a spreading plague had recently arrived,
And killed off all the seaweed; very little had survived.
'It came from over yonder,' and he pointed up ahead,
Along the very path her little group had planned to tread!

'If Paradise is what you seek, your road lies to the west,
For there you'll find a reef to more than satisfy your quest.
This valley leads to nothing more than darkness and despair.
Climb up across the mountains, for the land you seek lies there.'

Pearl thanked the Eel and took her leave, albeit with some care,
And joined her hidden comrades (and the Whale that wasn't there).
Then, taking heed of all they'd heard and what they hoped to find,
They started on the long, slow climb and left the Deep behind.

Scene II
The Source of the Poison

*In which the Soldiercrabs reach the end of their search,
Bert makes a shocking discovery, and Finneus reveals the
Grouper's treachery*

That night, as Pearl began to climb the Mountains of the Deep,
Her truelove, Bert, was woken from a restless, troubled sleep.
He fancied that he'd heard a cry come drifting on the tide,
And, pulling on four pairs of boots, he took a look outside.

The Soldiercrabs were camped upon a plain of withered stumps,
Once splendid coral sculptures, now just sticky, oily lumps.
For days the Crabs had marched across this grim, polluted land,
And Bert could tell the poison's source was very close at hand.

He peered into the murky gloom and listened for the sound,
Then faintly heard the cry again – his heart began to pound!
It came from somewhere up ahead, not far from where he stood,
So Bert went to investigate as all good soldiers should.

A rocky outcrop barred his way, demanding that he climb,
Through sickly streams of oily gunk and gobs of horrid slime.
He reached the crest and cried out with amazement and surprise,
For nothing could have steeled him for the sight that met his eyes.

A dozen massive canisters lay scattered on the ground,
Embedded in the blackened sand, with debris all around,
And from a drum that lay atop the huge, corroded heap,
He watched a stream of reeking, oily liquid slowly seep.

With horrid fascination Bert observed the poison flow,
Across the rocky landscape to the spreading plain below.
A figure lay upon the rocks; a spiky, yellow mane …
'It's Finneus!' Bert's urgent cry rang out across the plain.

He scrambled down into the slime and waded to his friend,
Who raised his head and pointed to the leaking barrel's end.
A tap protruding from the drum spewed forth the evil brew,
And, using his enormous brain, Bert knew just what to do.

He grabbed the tap and turned it off – but still the liquid flowed!
The toxic waste had caused the rubber washers to corrode.
Then, in a feat of wondrous strength, Bert raised his mighty claw,
And squeezed the rusty faucet till the poison flowed no more.

Bert's cry awoke the other Crabs, who scuttled up the hill,
And gathered round poor Finny, who was very gravely ill.
In fits and gasps he told them of the Grouper's shocking crime,
And how he'd tried to turn the tap and stop the deadly slime.

'My Catfish friends were captured by the Grouper's evil louts,
But I escaped and hunted for the Army's whereabouts.
I came across the poison and I tried to turn it off …'
His tale of woe was halted by an awful, racking cough.

The Soldiercrab Commander issued orders left and right:
'Take down the tents! Make fast the guns! We head for home tonight!
The enemy is elsewhere, though his crime is all around.
Leave not a stone or rock unturned – this Grouper must be found!'

Scene III
The Discovery of Paradise

*In which Pearl and her fellow travelers reach the end of their
climb and make a wonderful discovery*

For forty long, exhausting days and forty sleepless nights,
Pearl's little band climbed wearily to vast and giddy heights.
Where plankton swirled in drifting waves of phosphorescent snow,
The Seasnails plodded onwards through the strange, translucent glow.

They came across a meadow ringed by weird, exotic trees,
Where giant clumps of seaweed swayed upon the ocean breeze.
But ever upwards led the trail; they tarried but a day –
Pearl carved her secret sign and they continued on their way.

Eventually there came a day they climbed the final crest,
And gazed across a mighty plain that rolled into the west.
They'd reached the furthest threshold of the Continental Shelf,
And to their weary eyes it looked like Paradise itself.

The ocean gleamed and sparkled in the early morning light,
A grand, dramatic backdrop to a truly stirring sight.
For there beneath a gleaming veil of slanting, golden rays,
A coral reef of untold size lay glowing in the haze.

And, as they watched, it seemed to them the ocean rose and fell,
With countless tiny jewels that danced and flickered in the swell.
Pearl's eyes were filled with tears of joy; no further would they roam –
A million swirling Seahorses had come to guide them home.

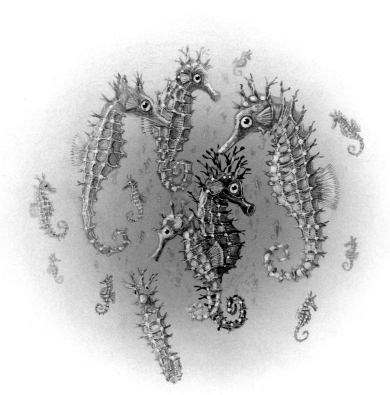

Scene IV
The End of the Grouper

*In which the Catfish are rescued, the Grouper is vanquished, and
Finny remembers something of great importance*

Behind the Grouper's Hide-out, in a dank and smelly shed,
The Catfish Gang lay bound and gagged, unhappy and unfed.
A week had passed and still no sign that help was on its way;
The gang's despondent mood increased with every passing day.

Then suddenly there came a mighty blow upon the door,
And through the splintered timbers crashed a massive, orange claw.
It smashed the door to smithereens, then disappeared from sight,
And left the Catfish speechless with astonishment and fright.

The claw belonged to Combat Lobster 46903,
The flagship of the Soldiercrabs' Crustacean Cavalry.
The Army had arrived at last, and leading the attack,
Was long-lost comrade Finneus, astride the Lobster's back!

The captive Catfish clapped and cheered, and danced in leaps and bounds,
Which seeing they were bound and gagged was harder than it sounds.
But then, as Finny freed his friends, they heard an angry shout:
The Grouper's thugs had heard the noise and come to check it out.

The Sharks converged on '903, who raised his giant claw,
And furnished Stan an uppercut beneath his greasy jaw.
The startled Sharks turned tail and fled, the Catfish giving chase,
But found themselves surrounded, fin to fin and face to face.

A cornered Shark is dangerous, as any Catfish knows,
And Finny quickly realized this scene could come to blows.
But just in time the Soldiercrabs arrived to save the day;
They apprehended Stan and Ted and marched them both away.

The Shark's arrest was carried out according to the book –
A routine operation: 'How to Bag a Petty Crook'.
But capturing the Swordfish, and his evil Grouper boss,
Was proving somewhat harder, and the Crabs were at a loss.

'Come out, and keep your fins held high!' the Crab Commander cried.
'We've got the place surrounded and we know that you're inside!'
But silence greeted every word the Colonel had to say –
Could Gropmund and his right-hand fish have somehow got away?

Then, with a roar, the Swordfish burst upon the startled Crabs,
And fiercely waved his sword about, with wicked sweeps and jabs.
He lunged towards the Colonel, dragged him roughly off his steed,
Then bit him on the ankle, which was very fierce indeed.

But Finny grabbed a lobster pot and rode into the fray,
And holding it above his head he shouted, 'Bombs Away!'
He trapped the Swordfish, sword and all, from snout to thrashing tail:
A neatly packaged villain in a private one-fish jail.

The Grouper watched the Swordfish fall and knew his race was run,
Then quoth aloud his Golden Rule: 'Look out for Number One!'
He grabbed a sack of unmarked pearls and quickly slipped outside,
But waiting there was Corporal Bert. 'You're through!' the Corporal cried.

He grabbed the squirming Grouper in his strong crustacean claws,
And carried him aloft amidst tumultuous applause.
And so the mighty Grouper fell, a sorry sight indeed:
Bereft of any dignity, a victim of his greed.

The Grouper's reign had ended, but his legacy remained.
They gazed across a barren land, a seascape cracked and stained.
The Army had prevailed and brought the villains to be tried,
But where were they to go, now that their coral reef had died?

Then Finny gave a sudden cry. Pearl's parting note to Bert!
He'd totally forgotten it, tucked deep beneath his shirt.
He drew it out, all stained and torn, but more or less complete,
And handed it to Bert, who read the precious, crumpled sheet.

'My Darling Bert, I write this with a sad and heavy heart,
For long and hard will be the days that we must be apart.
But, every turn my journey takes, a sign will mark the way,
For you to find and follow till we meet again one day.'

And so it was they learned about the trail Pearl left behind,
And followed in her footsteps, knowing not what they would find.
In time they reached the Promised Land and soon forgot their pain,
But nothing ever grew upon that coral reef again.

END OF ACT II

EPILOGUE
The New Seahorse Café

In which the New Seahorse Café is opened, and we learn the fate of the Grouper and his partners in crime

The Captain was a splendid sight: white glove and crimson vest,
A shiny golden medal gleaming brightly on his chest.
The medal read 'For Courage', and he glanced at it with pride,
Then squared his jaw, breathed deeply, checked his tie and stepped inside…

The café was a sea of fish, all dressed up to the nines,
A teeming mass of fins and flippers, earrings, spikes and spines.
As Bert stood gazing round the room, Pearl winked at him and smiled,
And served another customer a mug of Mollusc Mild.

Then Finneus called out his name. 'Come sit with us, my friend,
And let us toast the Hero of the Grouper's Dismal End!'
The Catfish Gang all stood and clapped, and Captain Bert went red.
'I only did my duty,' the embarrassed soldier said.

Young Finny had a medal, too: a Purple Heart and Rose,
That hung in pride of place upon his bruised and bandaged nose.
'In Grateful Recognition of a Brave and Wounded Trout' –
The glorious inscription dangled proudly from his snout.

The brand-new Seahorse Café had been open just a week,
But in that time the patronage had reached an all-time peak.
The techno-laser dance floor was awash with stomping feet,
As Kevin and the Kippers played their famous Reeftown Beat.

A backing group of Angelfish accompanied the band,
With perfect three-part harmonies, the finest in the land.
Since parting from the Grouper, they had polished up their act,
And now they filled the dance floor with the crowds they could attract.

The Grouper's Sharks were still around, a little short of friends,
But to their credit both of them had tried to make amends.
They worked the late-night roster, doing small domestic chores,
Collecting dirty glasses, washing walls and scrubbing floors.

Their former chief, the Swordfish, had a blossoming career,
That utilized his swordsmanship, at which he had no peer.
He peeled a mean potato, over eighty bags a week,
The fruit of hours of practice and a fabulous technique.

And as for Gropmund Grouper, undisputed king of crime,
He groveled at the kitchen sink, his flippers in the grime.
Beneath a pile of filthy plates, at last he understood,
That Greed Brought only Ruin, and the Tide had Turned for Good.

THE END

Library of Congress Cataloging-in-Publication Data
Base, Graeme.
The sign of the seahorse: a tale of greed and
high adventure in two acts/Graeme Base.
p.   cm.

Summary: The inhabitants of a coral reef are threatened when a
shady real estate deal started by the greedy Grouper floods their
area with poisonous waste.

ISBN 0−8109−3825−1
[1. Marine animals—Fiction. 2. Marine pollution—Fiction.
3. Pollution—Fiction. 4. Coral reefs and islands—Fiction.
5. Stories in rhyme.] I. Title.
PZB.3.B2894S1 1992   92−950
[Fic]—dc20

First published in 1992 by Penguin Books Australia Ltd.

Published in 1992 by Harry N. Abrams, Incorporated, New York
A Times Mirror Company

Printed and bound in the United States of America

THE NEW REEF

GREAT CONTINENTAL

THE
MOUNTAINS
OF
THE
DEEP

THE OLD REEF

The
Army
Barracks

Grouper's
Diner

The
Seahorse
Café

REEFTOWN

The
Wreck